A Study-Group Success Story

Best Practices from Our Give & Grow Group's First 20 Years Together

Ron Greenberg, CLU®, AEP®
Brian Heckert, CLU®, ChFC®, QPFC, AIF®
Peter Maller, MBA, CFP®, AEP®
John Moshides, CLU®, ChFC®, AEP®, CLTC®
Bryan Sweet, CLU®, ChFC®, AIF®

The contents of this book are not meant to serve as advice related to any securities or investment transactions but are offered as a road map to success that an individual can achieve as a member of a study group. Any reference to individual relationships with our broker dealers is for their compliance and to indicate our respect for the role they play in keeping our firms compliant with the regulations we face.

Published in the United States of America

ISBN-13: 978-1987415681

ISBN-10: 198741568X

What's Inside...

INTRODUCTION:
Your Study Group Is Your Tribe

> "Don't downgrade your dream just to fit your reality. Upgrade your conviction to match your destiny."
> —Author Unknown

Since the dawn of time, tribes have gathered and shared ideas to help their communities survive and prosper. Over campfires during the times of early *Homo sapiens* to the modern-day boardrooms of large corporations, gathering to share ideas has proven to make groups stronger.

In *The Rational Optimist*, Matt Ridley presents the power of sharing ideas and commerce: "Modern philosophers who aspire to rise above the sordid economic reality of the world would do well to recall that this trade made possible the cross-fertilization of ideas that led to great discoveries."[1]

---

1. Matt Ridley, *The Rational Optimist: How Prosperity Evolves* (New York: P.S./ HarperCollins Publishers, 2011), 171.

Today we can meet and discuss ideas with others from around the world in a matter of minutes. Ideas are shared across waves of light, not just the glow of a campfire. And our clients and prospects demand more because they, too, can access more.

Historically, only those who could read had access to information. Early cave dwellers shared by telling stories and then by writing. As communication and language developed, those who could read and write controlled the access. In the Dark Ages, those with access to books controlled the sharing of information. Now, with the internet mostly free and available to much of the world's population, information is free, but the sharing of accurate information is clouded by the noise of propaganda and outright inaccurate information. This is where a study group brings value to participants and their clientele.

With easy and cheap access to data, it is imperative that financial advisors stay at the cutting edge of the information curve to deliver accurate and relevant

information to clients based on a group evaluation of accuracy of that information. In effect, a study group brings together the best of the face-to-face storytelling over the campfires of our ancestors with the most advanced technology of today.

As financial advisors, we are under pressure to meet activity demands to produce a certain amount of business. Usually, this crowds out the time left for self-improvement. Taking time out of our busy schedules to attend another vendor meeting gives us the false impression that we are learning, but often the learning is geared to a single vendor or product. An effective study group alleviates this problem by bringing the vendor to the member, and the group controls the content and the questions. This produces a better and more open dialogue than attending their meeting, where they control the message.

A study group allows advisors to join a small, friendly gathering for sharing, allowing a more intimate delivery from that advisor than would be possible if the advisor had given a talk in front of a large group. Our study group gives us time away from the office and phones so that ideas and concepts sink in and simmer without those pressures distracting from the impact of the messages we hear. It also allows the conversations and the idea sharing to continue throughout the day and into the evening. The collaborative group setting is where the most insightful ideas are born. Your study group is your tribe!

Your study group is your tribe!

This book is for those who want to grow and expand and become the best they can be. We have given you a road map of how study groups can be part of that process. We strongly believe there is zero downside to starting a study group and a huge upside to at least trying it. If you're going to try it, why not follow a road map of best practices to help you be more successful and learn from things that went well with our group over the past twenty years? We hope this book helps you get your study group off the ground so that you, too, can enjoy the benefits we have gained from our group.

We hope you enjoy the book and that it inspires you to launch your own study group.

CHAPTER 1

About the Give & Grow Study Group

> "Four short words sum up what has lifted most successful individuals above the crowd: a little bit more. They did all that was expected of them and a little bit more."
>
> —A. Lou Vickery

Ron Greenberg started his career in the Prudential agency system and heard of a few experienced advisors who were participating in something they called a "study group." At the time, Ron didn't know what that meant; perhaps it was a handful of agents who got together and studied various aspects of the business in a group setting?

When he spoke with one of those advisors, however, Ron learned that the study-group concept was about sharing ideas and best practices with each other. The gist was to be able to pick the brains of others who shared the same values, ethics, and passion for the business. Ron had been in the business for about ten years at that time and had experienced some success but wanted more…much more.

So began his search for the right study group.

We were all members of the Million Dollar Round Table (MDRT). Ron reached out to someone at MDRT headquarters to develop a list of potential candidates who met the criteria he wanted in the members of his group. And that is how we all met.

The driving force behind our study-group model has always been that we come from a place of abundance and are always looking for ways to pay it forward. That is a big part of why we wanted to write this book. We think every budding entrepreneur can benefit from the study-group model, and we have captured for you in this book the best practices we've used as a foundation for our study group.

Our Measurable Improvements

If you are unsure about the power of bringing a small group of individuals together to further their success, consider the following numbers. Here is a brief snapshot of where things stood for the five members of our group, collectively, when we started the group in 1998, compared to where we were in 2015, after eighteen years in the study group.

	In 1998	In 2017
Gross dealer concession (GDC)	$1.1 million	$15.1 million
Full-time employees	20	58
Designations	5	15
Assets under management (AUM)	$1 million	$2.53 billion

We all believe strongly that we would not have achieved anywhere close to that type of growth if we had worked alone, without the benefit of the group.

The Past Twenty Years: Our Personal Reflections and Biggest Takeaways

Collectively, the five members of our group have gained tremendous personal and professional benefit from the Give & Grow Study Group. Individually, we have grown our practices well beyond the level of success we could have accomplished on our own.

Forming our Give & Grow Study Group in 1998 is one of the best decisions we have ever made. Below are some personal reflections that describe the significant role the group has played in our businesses and lives.

Ronald J. Greenberg, CLU®, AEP®

Founding Partner
Greenberg & Rapp Financial Group, Inc.
M Holdings Securities, Inc.[2]
East Hanover, New Jersey

Number of employees: 16 full-time
AUM: ~ $650 million
GDC: ~ $3 million
Insurance revenue: ~ $2 million

Since the inception of our study group, I have received immense value in all facets of my business. The group has been my sounding board and advisory "committee" for many decisions over the years, helping me grow and make key decisions and providing guidance when needed. Imagine having four like-minded business owners in your industry willing to share everything about what they do and how they do it, holding nothing back. This is the kind of open relationship we

The group has been my sounding board.

2. Please see the broker dealer disclaimers on page 84.

have cultivated over the past twenty years as we have all experienced exponential growth.

Here are just a few of my biggest takeaways from the group—implementable ideas I learned from the group that have led to significant improvements in my practice:

1. Every morning, I have a "daily huddle" with my administrative assistant. We meet for five or ten minutes to discuss the biggest priorities for the day. This has made a big difference in the way we work together, and it keeps the daily interruptions from taking our focus off the important tasks for the day.

2. We hired a personnel consultant, Lauren Farasati, who spoke to us during one of our study-group meetings. She analyzed our business and was instrumental in helping us get the right people in the right roles—or, in the words of author Jim Collins, to make sure we had "the right people in the right seats on the bus." She helped ensure that we gave the right people the opportunity to succeed in my practice. We hired her at a time when the practice

was growing, and her guidance enabled us to enhance the caliber of the talent on our team.

3. We hired another consultant who spoke to our group, a specialist named Phil Palaveev. He is well known in the financial services industry and is president of The Ensemble Practice in Seattle. He helped us develop a compensation and bonus structure for our entire organization.

Brian D. Heckert, CLU®, ChFC®, QPFC, AIF®

CEO and Founder
Financial Solutions Midwest, LLC
Kestra Investment Services, LLC [3]
Nashville, Illinois

Number of employees: 8
(7 full-time, 1 part-time)
AUM: ~$370 million
GDC: ~$1.4 million,
including insurance

The group environment and accountability have been the driving force in my progress toward becoming a better advisor and a better person. The group's values align with my vision of what the perfect advisor should be. But what makes this experience most effective is the absolute sharing from those who practice daily what it takes to be the best. Our combined exposure to meetings and interactions throughout this profession multiplies the ideas fivefold. Our friendship has grown through this process as our businesses have expanded, making this the perfect format for helping each other while helping ourselves.

Here are just three of my biggest takeaways from the group—implementable ideas I learned from the group that have led to significant improvements in my practice:

1. In 2004, the revenues generated in my practice had taken a considerable shift. The study-group members

---

3. Please see the broker dealer disclaimers on page 84.

helped me address my cash-flow needs to prevent serious financial damage. After review of our personal financial plans with the entire group, we would spend time critiquing and commenting on each other's plans. After I presented, the group helped me focus on ways to illuminate unnecessary business and the debt associated with it. It was like having a board of directors provide me with outside advice and comments while looking at my best interests in ways that I could not have done on my own.

2. In 2008, I met economic writer Jeffery Saut, Chief Economist from Raymond James, through our group. His economic writings have provided me with valuable insight into market trends that translate into market recommendations we make for our clients. He provides one voice and one source for unbiased information through a clear vision of how the markets work. We've been able to incorporate his observations into developing our own portfolio strategies. This is the biggest advantage of having members from multiple broker dealers in the same group who openly share resources with the other members.

> The group helped me focus on ways to illuminate unnecessary business.

3. A third specific takeaway was the introduction of the Sherman Sheet. We use the Sherman Sheet in ways that other members of the group do not. It's an example of how to take a tool and have other people adjust it and use it in their own practices and then improve the benefit to the entire group via group share. Everybody brings their best idea to the table and openly shares the resources they use with their own client base.

Peter D. Maller, MBA, CFP®, AEP®

Founder and President
Maller Wealth Advisors, Inc.
Lincoln Financial Advisors [4]
Hunt Valley, Maryland

Number of employees: 24 (16
full-time, 8 part-time)
AUM: $800 million
GDC: $5.5 million

In this Give & Grow Study Group, there has been full engagement and dedication by the five members. No one misses a meeting, and everyone is always ultra-prepared with their homework assignments, as well as with scenarios they are wanting/willing to share.

During the meetings, open and honest feedback and suggestions are always given in a manner that truly helps the person in question. Those discussions are then reinforced by follow-up and accountability. I can lean on my "brothers" for anything business- or personal-related and know that the feedback I get is from their hearts! We care greatly about one another, and a victory or loss for one person is a victory or loss that the rest of the group shares collectively, with compassion.

We have pushed each other to be premier leaders in the financial services industry, as well as in other aspects of our lives. We realize that we all need balance among work, marriage, spirituality, fatherhood, exercise, health, and having fun.

Here are just a few of my biggest takeaways from the group—implementable ideas I learned from the group that have led to significant improvements in my practice:

1. The general great ideas and strategies employed by the various members in different economic, investment, and legal environments

2. The intellectual capital and mind-sets gained from members through their participation in coaching programs over the years

4. Please see the broker dealer disclaimers on page 84.

3. The focus on overall lifestyle (work–life balance), which is a focus of, and common topic with, this group

4. Having my fellow members serve as a sounding board for business and personal issues that come up from time to time

5. Learning about the different business structures and foci of the members…although they are all different, they are all successful

John C. Moshides, CLU®, ChFC®, AEP®, CLTC®

Financial Services Executive
President, Moshides Financial Group
Creator of The Wealth Management
  Process™ and The Business of Wealth
MML Investors Services, LLC [5]
Amherst, New York

> Number of employees: 7 (5 full-time, 2 part-time)
> AUM: ~$260 million
> GDC: ~$1.4 million

Most businesses are very protective of their intellectual property and personal success and often employ attorneys to protect their "trade secrets" so others cannot use them or call them their own. The members of our study group are the antithesis of this type of thinking. Our members have taken our practices to levels we could have never thought possible when we first came together as a group twenty years ago.

> Our guys cannot wait to share with each other whatever concept or break-through we have experienced.

The difference is, our guys cannot wait to share with each other whatever concept or break-through we have experienced so we can all

5. Please see the broker dealer disclaimers on page 84.

improve and continue down the road of the endless pursuit of excellence. The goal has always been and always will be to remain client-centric…what can we do to better serve our clients with black-belt services while creating a positive environment for our employee/associates to be compensated fairly, grow professionally, and have a lot of fun along the way?

We are also aware that if the previous falls into place, then we, the advisors, will be rewarded properly as well. Success does not come without a bit of pain and suffering along the way, and the men who make up our group are always there to tell each other what we *need* to hear, not always what we *want* to hear! I am so very proud of what we have all accomplished and the relationships we have developed. I know I can call Brian, Ron, Peter, and Bryan with whatever challenge or problem I have (both professionally and personally), and they will always be there with great advice and with my best interest in mind!

Here are just a few of my biggest takeaways from the group—implementable ideas I learned from the group that have led to significant improvements in my practice:

1. I have learned to step outside my comfort zone and think bigger than I ever would have on my own. The group has both motivated me and given me the confidence to achieve things I may never have done

13

without their bold thinking, encouragement, and inspiration.

2. As I have tried new things, the group has always been a sounding board with heavy-handed constructive critiquing, which one needs from time to time—tough love!

3. We always bring perspective to each other. I might see it one way, and someone else might see it totally differently. But after good, collaborative discussion, we usually gain great clarity on an issue.

Bryan J. Sweet, CLU®, ChFC®, MSFS, CFS®

Founder and CEO, Sweet Financial
   Services
Wealth Advisor, Raymond James
   Financial Services
Raymond James Financial Services, Inc. [6]
Creator of The Dream Architect™
Cofounder of Dare to Dream Enterprises
Creator of Elite Wealth Advisor
   Symposium
Fairmont, Minnesota

Number of employees: 14 full-time
AUM: ~$450 million
GDC: ~$3.8 million, including insurance

    Joining this group has truly been one of the best decisions I've made in my career. I have gained four great confidants/friends/like-minded entrepreneurs who push each other to be their best but also challenge every decision to make sure it's the right one.

    Being a member of this group has forced me to think outside the box. I have gained ideas from my fellow members' different perspectives because each is from a

---

6. Please see the broker dealer disclaimers on page 84.

different broker dealer and in a different part of the country. All of us would do anything to help another, whether on a business or personal issue. Other than PEAK, Strategic Coach, and the Genius Network, this is the most impactful group in propelling my career.

Here are just a few of my biggest takeaways from the group—implementable ideas I learned from the group that have led to significant improvements in my practice:

> All of us would do anything to help another.

1. The group decided to write a book together. Going through that process gave me the confidence to write additional books for Sweet Financial Services and Dare to Dream Enterprises. Without that experience, I probably would have never written the books. As a result of publishing those books, amazing by-products are coming to both businesses.

2. Lauren Farasati, a team and staffing expert, spoke at one of our meetings. I hired her to make some improvements in our office. Working with Lauren, the

biggest breakthrough was that our director of operations was moving, and we needed to find a replacement.

We tried everything but couldn't find anyone. Lauren ultimately recommended that we promote our client-service person, Brittany, to be our new director. That has been one of the most impactful decisions I've ever made because Brittany has been extremely beneficial in creating a culture of excellence for our practice, and she has an amazing entrepreneurial mind. Brittany and I are now partners in a separate business together and are developing multiple programs that generate hundreds of thousands of dollars of revenue (soon, potentially millions).

3. I recently sponsored an Elite Wealth Advisor symposium, which was an invitation-only event for seventy-five advisors. I had to create three days of content and speakers that would amaze and delight very successful people. Because of the growth of each member of our study group, I proudly asked each of them to speak to this distinguished audience. All of them contributed greatly to the event being an unbelievable success.

The Group, Then and Now

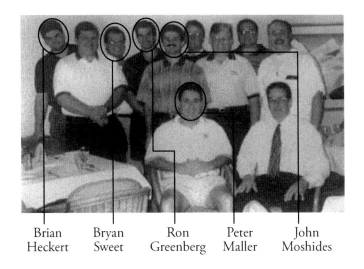

Brian   Bryan   Ron   Peter   John
Heckert   Sweet   Greenberg   Maller   Moshides

This photo was taken on January 18, 2018, during the group's meeting in Miami. From left are Brian Heckert, Ron Greenberg, Peter Maller, Bryan Sweet, and John Moshides.

CHAPTER 2

The Benefits of a Study Group

> "An arrow can only be shot by pulling it backwards. So when life is dragging you back with difficulties, it means that it's going to launch you into something great."
> —Author Unknown

A study group is composed of peers who care about common concerns. The group essentially becomes a "brain trust" where we all share ideas to help each other grow. We strongly feel that, no matter what stage you are at in your business, you are never good enough to stop learning from others.

When people ask why we want to share the story of how our study group was formed, we point directly to the personal and professional successes we have all experienced. Before we had the benefit of the supportive environment that a study group provides, our financial practices were very small compared to what they are today.

In this chapter are some of the key benefits of being in a study group. They constitute the reasons we feel everyone should be part of a study group.

Accountability

We all know how important accountability is in the insurance and financial services industry. Just as advisors benefit from being held accountable for their daily, weekly, and quarterly activity, leaders need to be held accountable for goals, objectives, and improvement for their firms. This is especially important in the early years.

> Leaders need to be held accountable for goals, objectives, and improvement.

We push each other to aim higher and work harder. We incorporated a saying into the group: "Don't just say it; do it."

Also, being members of the group keeps our focus on the right things. We've all observed successful folks in our industry who increase their lifestyles commensurate with their increases in income. At times, their lifestyles might even exceed their incomes. The group has helped us stick to the fundamentals and not get caught up in a focus on material things.

Part of our philosophy has always been, regardless of how successful we are, to make sure we're being good savers. We remind one another, "Let's make sure we are living within our means, and let's make sure we are diversified." We always ensure that we have proper insurance in place.

When we take care of these important financial matters, we are better professionals. We will be more effective with our clients if our own financial houses are in order.

We made financial accountability a part of our study

group so none of us would fall into the trap of leveraging our futures with loans, credit cards, and houses that are too big and leases on cars that are too expensive.

Increased Engagement

Study groups are a hallmark of the financial services industry, and they are an integral part of many university programs as well.

Richard J. Light, PhD, is the Carl H. Pforzheimer, Jr., Professor of Teaching and Learning at the Harvard Graduate School of Education. In 1986, Harvard University president Derek Bok asked Dr. Light to find out what indicator best showed whether a student would succeed or fail. Dr. Light's research team discovered that creating or joining study groups was the best indicator of success. Students who participated in study groups were more engaged in what they did, were better prepared for class, and learned significantly more than those who studied alone. They even had more fun![7]

> It's an incredibly fun process that keeps you consistently engaged.

We couldn't agree more. When you are focused on improving your own business by learning from others while also sharing your best practices, it's an incredibly fun process that keeps you consistently engaged.

Better Client Experiences

You might think the main benefit of joining a study group is the increased money it can bring you as you grow your business. Although that has been a nice by-product of our

---

7. "Encouraging Study Groups," Brigham Young University Center for Teaching and Learning, http://ctl.byu.edu/tip/encouraging-study-groups.

study group, we formed our group to improve our clients' experiences in working with us. We have all been willing to spend money, time, and effort to make the client experience better because we know the end result will be increased client retention, which results in higher revenue for our firms.

In fact, our main focus isn't on us, but rather on others—on the clients we serve—and how we can improve so we can do more for them. Ultimately, the focus we keep on our clients is what has led to our success.

This philosophy is the core of who we are as a group. We all want each other to be wildly successful, and we push each other to do our best for our clients. In the end, that is a big part of why it's been so rewarding for all of us.

Personal and Professional Support

Our Give & Grow Study Group isn't just about our professional lives. We take a holistic approach to sharing important aspects of our personal and professional lives. We spend a lot of time in the study group discussing diet, health, and marriage. It's about all aspects of our well-being, not just making more money.

We all know that personal difficulties can affect our work, and vice versa. Having the support of like-minded colleagues who share similar values and goals is priceless.

On the professional side, belonging to the group has also helped each of us work though ceilings of complexity. We've all had issues with this as we grew our companies, and we've been able to talk through them and help each other. We have helped each other make decisions in specific cases. When one of us asks, "How do you solve a client problem?" the other group members offer their suggestions. It is a great resource for solving issues we can't solve easily on our own.

> It is a great resource for solving issues.

Our Own Personal Board of Directors

Imagine that every time you have a question about a specific process or strategy in your business, you had several close colleagues to ask for guidance and feedback. Instead of trying to figure out everything yourself, you have access to, in essence, your own personal board of directors to consult at any time. This informal board of directors serves as a reliable sounding board for questions, concerns, and ideas.

Think about some of the questions you might bounce off a group of peers in your same business without fear of competition:

1. Has anyone ever thought about going into the _____ part of the business?

2. What do you pay your COO?

3. Can you share your job descriptions for your key staff?

4. When was the last time you needed to fire someone? How did you handle it?

5. When searching for a _____, what has given you the best results? Search firm? Job search engine? Can you share your job postings with me?

6. I'm having trouble convincing a client that he should purchase a _____ plan. Have you ever had a similar challenge? What did you do? What worked, and what didn't work? What lessons did you learn from that experience?

7. I'm having trouble getting some of my key employees to think and behave like owners; I want our interests to be aligned. Have you implemented anything that has worked or not worked?

As a business owner, who can you approach to ask these types of questions? A business coach might help, but you cannot buy the type of advice and the sharing of experience and strategies that fellow business owners can bring to the table in a study group. You could ask colleagues, but if they are in the same market as you are, you risk sharing valuable information with a competitor.

Besides the obvious financial rewards and camaraderie you receive from starting a study group, there are many benefits you might not have considered.

Honest Feedback

Because all of us are leaders in our respective firms, we can sometimes fall into what we call the "trap of leadership." If you are the boss, your team tends to go along with you rather than questioning your ideas. If you come up with a questionable idea, they are going to support you, for the most part, no matter what.

Part of the power of study-group collaboration is that we challenge each other. We can voice our honest opinions because we do not depend on one another for a paycheck. The honest feedback we get in the group gives us perspectives from our peers. It forces us to think about decisions we're pursuing in the presence of people who care about us but also challenge us to reach higher than we would on our own. That is a benefit that you can't get anywhere else.

> "That which does not challenge you does not change you."
> —Ron's Personal Trainer

Self-Managed Companies

Another benefit the study group provides is that it allows us to create "self-managed companies." This means we no longer have to watch over every aspect of our businesses on a daily basis because we have empowered our teams to step up and take ownership of the work they perform.

A Nudge Outside Our Comfort Zones

One of the biggest benefits is how the group forces us out of our comfort zones—everyone needs that to grow. We all need to have that uncomfortable feeling if we are to grow. Without the group's support, our tendency would be to pull back from that feeling. Instead, we embrace it and help each other get through it, and we are better businessmen and leaders as a result.

One thing the group does that is extremely helpful is encourage everyone to think bigger. When we first started, we had what we thought at the time were big goals but now are very small in comparison to how big we think today. A study group pushes you to think much bigger than you ever could on your own. We take on projects like writing books and speaking on panels, which ensures that we are always learning and growing.

Team Growth

Another possibly underappreciated benefit to a study group is team growth. When we all started, we each had two or three people working for us, and today we have well-established firms and businesses. As a result of creating self-managing companies, we are all able to take a lot of time away from our offices to think about our businesses and work *on* them instead of always working *in* them.

Even now, twenty years in, we are still growing, evolving, and learning from the group. In fact, each of us is forming sub-study groups within our own firms. Our COOs are forming study groups, as are people who do underwriting. Even though you probably won't create sub-study groups right away, it's important to note that the group can evolve as you evolve.

> Each of us is forming sub-study groups within our own firms.

Lifestyle Improvements

Another huge benefit is that we've all had tremendous lifestyle improvements. Because of the group, we have traveled to all sorts of places in the United States and around the world that we may not have otherwise gotten to visit.

Access to Speakers and Resources

Another benefit is gaining access to speakers and resources that we, on our own, would either not have been aware of or would not have been able to get access to ourselves cost-effectively. We have all learned about resources and speakers we wouldn't have been familiar with if we were working on our own.

Friendship

You don't really think about this when you're starting a study group, but we have created some great friendships within our group. It has turned into a small brotherhood.

As you can see, the benefits you can derive personally and professionally by being a member of a study group are priceless. We have grown far more by being a part of this group than we could have ever grown working as silos.

CHAPTER 3

How to Start Your Own Study Group

If there isn't a study group in your area or company that you feel would benefit you, think about starting your own. When you launch your own group, you have the advantage of structuring the group the way you envision it. You have control over all aspects of the group's membership and focus.

Here are some guidelines we recommend for starting your group, based on our experience.

Seek Members with Similar Values, Goals, and Business Experience

Before you decide to start a study group, think about your personal values, goals, and objectives. What do you want to get out of participation in a study group? What are you hoping to accomplish? Understanding what you want out of a group is imperative to a successful experience.

It's also critical to find out what other potential members of the study group would like to get out of the group as well. The more closely your values, goals, and objectives are aligned, the more successful your study group will be. Are the

29

potential members' attitudes toward family life and business life compatible? The group doesn't have to be homogeneous, but it helps if you have commonality regarding what is and is not acceptable so the group can flourish.

One of the reasons we believe we've been so successful is that, right from the get-go, we considered it important for all the study-group members to be within a reasonable age range (we are all within ten years of each other), to have similar business experience, and to have similar levels of productivity. We figured that if we were going to be in the trenches together, helping our businesses grow, we should all start out in similar positions.

Starting out from similar vantage points is important.

Starting out from similar vantage points is important because as your study-group members' businesses grow and evolve, the group will, too. We have gone from pure growth mode to business-development mode to legacy-planning mode.

Earlier in our careers, we focused heavily on sales mastery, which was mostly about sales ideas and techniques.

Then our focus moved to business ideas and business development as our sales processes became very successful. We also focused on business management—how to hire, fire, build an office, and manage technology. The last phase is legacy planning, when we plan for the later stages of our business cycles and bring in junior advisors. We plan for endeavors and processes that are much bigger than the individuals in the group.

> We are all moving into legacy-planning mode now.

Because we all joined the group at a similar phase of our lives and careers, we've all grown together, and we are all moving into legacy-planning mode now.

Seek Members from Different Geographic Locations

We recommend that every member of your study group live in different communities or geographic locations. It is difficult to be open and honest about your business strategies when someone in the group is competing with you directly for market share.

We started out with members from the East Coast and the West Coast. Now, many years later, we are all pretty much located on the East Coast and in the Midwest. That helps a lot in terms of communicating across time zones and travel convenience. We think it has been optimal for us not to be too spread out around the country, although that was the case in the beginning. Time is our most valuable and precious commodity. With all of us relatively close to each other, we do not waste too much time traveling to meet with or see each other.

Seek Members with Different Company Affiliations

Some carriers—for example, Guardian, New York Life, and Northwestern Mutual®— have formed study groups of advisors within their own companies. There are clearly benefits to having a group in which all participants work under the same platform or for the same company. Brainstorming and developing ideas to improve products, marketing, design, and service to "the field" can be valuable.

However, if all your study-group members are part of the same platform or company, you might spend too much time discussing "politics" and issues within that system and not enough time on growing your businesses. For that reason, we suggest that you avoid having multiple members who are from the same

> Avoid having multiple members who are from the same broker dealers or insurance companies.

32

broker dealers or insurance companies. We have found it to be much more invigorating and educational to learn from people who bring different perspectives from their different companies or broker dealers. It has been a tremendous benefit for Give & Grow members to hear and see what each of our platforms/companies do. Being exposed to different ways of doing things has led to changes that we have taken back to our respective corporate headquarters for implementation.

Because we do not compete in the same markets, it has been easier and more natural for us to share openly, and we feel less inhibited about revealing our strategies and metrics. We are all from different geographic areas and different broker dealers. We all agree that we might be less apt to share as openly as we have if one of the group members were competing across the street or around the block from us.

Having some commonality among members is important, though. Being able to understand and relate to what each member is doing and what you are striving to improve is important. We each have slightly different practice specialties in our group. We have built and grown our respective practices and expertise through feedback from each other, as well as from outside coaches and mentors.

There are pros and cons to both concepts. Think about your personal needs and objectives before deciding which is most beneficial to you.

Cast Your Net Nationally

As mentioned earlier, we wanted the members of Give & Grow to be within the same age range, the same income bracket, the same number of years in the business—within five to ten years or so—and to be located within a reasonable distance of each other.

For your group, look to *national* industry organizations. *Local or regional* organizations won't give you a wide enough

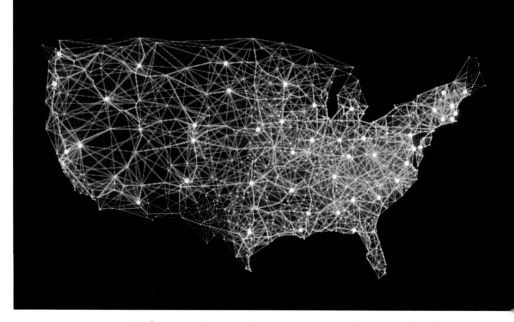

scope. To form a robust study group, you need to get a broad spectrum of input and advice. Having group members from different backgrounds, different companies, and different parts of the country is ideal.

This diversity not only gives you the unique perspective of professionals from other areas, but there is a practical consideration as well: we share everything—marketing ideas, sales concepts, client-acquisition strategies, and retention techniques. We don't want to share these best practices openly with people who compete in our own backyards.

There is some trial and error involved in organizing a group like this.

Please note that there is some trial and error involved in organizing a group like this. It will be challenging to come out of the gate with a perfect collection of the right people. But if you devote the time and effort early on, hopefully you will have a good core group to build on.

Require a Strong Commitment to the Group

We believe everyone in any study group should have a strong commitment to the group. In the twenty years we've been meeting, we can count on one hand the number of times someone has had to miss a meeting. We want a 100 percent commitment from every member.

We knew from the beginning that we had to commit to coming to every meeting to support each other, or it wasn't going to work. We felt so strongly about this that we made it a rule that if someone had to miss a meeting, he had to pay his share anyway. We wanted a full commitment from everyone so that we all could get the most benefit from each other.

If even one member of the group fails to make the group's collective success a priority, then the entire group will suffer. We all come to the meetings very well prepared. We know that if everybody embraces the philosophy of giving value, then all of us will get a lot out of it.

> We found five to eight members to be the ideal size for a study group.

Strive for Five to Eight Members

Although you can make a case for larger groups, we found five to eight members to be the ideal size for a study group. Too many participants bring too many challenges and scheduling conflicts. Also, the meetings could go on for too long with everybody chiming in and providing their input. Less than five people is probably too small, but we think that more than eight people is too big.

You might need to start with a larger group so that you end up with this ideal number. Our experience tells us that over time, a few folks won't fit in and will need to leave the group.

Designate a Leader

To get a study group off the ground, there has to be an initiator, a de facto initial "leader" of the group who helps pull it together. Hopefully, that individual will be you. The leader will write a letter introducing himself and welcoming members to the group. Although we've never had any hierarchy to our group beyond getting it off the ground, one person needs to step up in the early stages and provide leadership.

> One person needs to step up in the early stages and provide leadership.

There is a fair amount of initial start-up organization: determining when and where to have the first meeting, setting the agenda, handling the details of both the business and social sides of the meeting, etc. It is critical that the first meeting be well organized because it will set the tone for the future of the group.

Send Out Introduction Letters

Once you have identified potential members you want to invite to be part of the group, send out an introduction letter to each candidate. In it, state the purpose of the group, its collective goals and objectives, and expectations of members. Ask the potential members to respond with their level of interest by a specified date.

In general, this letter should convey the group's broad game plan and what the group hopes to achieve. Prospective members receiving this letter should share the vision and be ready to attend the first meeting with enthusiasm.

Establish Rules of Engagement

For a group to be successful, there must be rules of engagement that everybody understands and agrees to follow. If there are no rules that define the group's mission and objectives, it will be confusing, and you might run into problems.

> There must be rules of engagement.

The first two rules of engagement for our group are "You have to give" and "You need to be in growth mode." Those are the two absolute, unequivocal bylaws that will never change unless we decide to change them. What this means is that we are all giving and sharing, and if any group member is not, then this is not the place for him. Don't come to a meeting if you are not looking to grow, excel, and give!

The Option to Merge Two Groups

We didn't merge two groups, but it's worth mentioning because we have seen other groups merge. In one case, we saw a study group with years of business experience establish a mentoring relationship with a younger study group. We've also seen three or four situations in which older, more mature study groups didn't necessarily want to bring young

professionals into the group who were in different phases of their businesses and lives, so they developed mentoring relationships. The groups with older members would mentor groups with members who were ten, fifteen, or twenty years younger.

They have held their meetings around the same time for a number of years so they can do some common things together and share ideas with the younger groups.

Although we haven't done this yet, we have discussed sharing resources with other study groups. We would not attend meetings together, but we would meet in the same locations for the purpose of sharing the cost of outside speakers. This would enable us to bring in higher-quality speakers. We haven't chosen to do this mainly because we have been willing to shoulder more of the cost ourselves so that we can have meetings in which we can be more candid and open within the group that is familiar to us.

> **We have discussed sharing resources with study groups.**

Adding and Removing Members

Often in study groups, it becomes necessary to add members to the group or remove members from the group. Through some trial and error, we now have a process to follow when we consider bringing people into our study group. We call them "interviewees."

Typically, the way this works is that our group members will suggest certain people who might be a good fit for Give & Grow. We have a general conversation about who those potential members are, and then we invite them to a meeting so we can interview them, get to know them, and see if they might fit in with our group, culture-wise.

For the interview, we ask each interviewee to describe his operation, work structure, and the way he operates his business. We want to make sure new members have fairly substantial and established businesses. We also ask interviewees to present on a given topic or two. We want to see how well they interact with the group. In other words, we want to make sure they don't come just to sit around and watch what we do. They have to make a presentation to the group and show us something of value that they can contribute and that we could expect from them in the future. This helps us determine their capacity to do that.

> We want to make sure new members have fairly substantial and established businesses.

Another step that is very helpful in the process of determining whether people are a good fit—and this wasn't necessarily our intention—is to see them operate outside the study-group environment, at dinners and recreational activities. By including them in these activities, we've learned a lot in every instance.

Our study group has an all-or-nothing vote on adding

new members. In other words, we all must agree that we want to bring a new member in, or it's a no. All of us have friends we think would be compatible, but it's a hard thing to add somebody after we've been meeting for twenty years already. Having a process through which you interview potential members is key. Bring them to one of your meetings, see what they have to add to the group, and find out how they can increase the value of the group.

> Our study group has an all-or-nothing vote on adding new members.

We started with eleven members and whittled the number down to the five we have now. It's better to start with a bigger group and pare it down to those who fit than to try to add more members later. As you work together and grow together, you come to understand each other well. That makes it hard for somebody who comes in five or ten years later to establish the same type of rapport with the original members because they don't have that same long-term relationship.

It's also important to have a process for removing members. Unfortunately, we have had to ask people to leave our group. It's never a fun decision. It usually happens when an advisor reaches the point in his life when he isn't growing anymore or the direction of his firm is different than that of the other group members. When this has happened, we have simply asked the member to leave and given our reason. Thankfully, they have all flourished after leaving because they wanted to go in different directions than we were going, so it worked out for them as well.

We can say without hesitation that starting your own study group with like-minded colleagues from different geographic areas and different companies can be one of the most rewarding experiences you have ever had. There really is no downside. If you start a group and it doesn't work out, try to discover what went wrong. Then try again, using different parameters. Keep trying because we are certain the reward will far outweigh your effort.

CHAPTER 4

How to Plan a Study-Group Meeting

"Life is about deferred penalties and deferred rewards."
—John C. Moshides

Planning your study-group meetings should be given the priority it deserves. It is important to host a useful, enjoyable meeting for your fellow group members. Plus, there is an unwritten rule that you do not want to be the one who hosts the worst study-group meeting, or what's perceived as the worst. It has always been our experience that we try to "one-up" the one who went before, which we'll admit is tough to keep up.

The daily grind of what we do and the busy travel schedules all lead to the temptation and potential to give the planning less than our full attention. But planning a study-

group meeting should come with the same kind of emphasis that we give a client meeting or seminar for our clients. Attention to detail should be of the utmost importance.

The amount of prep work we do prior to our meetings is immense. And then when the meeting begins, we do have a lot of fun, but they start early and end late. We work really, really hard. Everyone takes the meetings very seriously.

Our meetings tend to run for two to three days, depending on the type of meeting. For example, for the meeting we attended while writing this book, we all flew in on a Monday and had no real business responsibility other than to meet for dinner Monday evening, catch up a bit, and get the ideas flowing. Then we worked hard most of Tuesday. The only real time off was about an hour for lunch.

When to Meet

During our first two years, we tried to meet three times per year but quickly realized that was too many meetings, based on the travel required and the demands of our members' practices. So we determined early on that we wanted to limit our meetings to twice a year.

We meet early in the year, around March, in a location with a warm climate to evaluate our goals. Our second meeting is six months later, in September, to report on our progress. This has worked well for our group because all of us tend to be in areas where winter affects us somewhat negatively. There is no reason your meetings couldn't be at other times of the year; this is just what has worked well for us.

We don't have a rule about when our meetings are held. It varies from meeting to meeting, based on what we all have going on. When we first established the group, we held our meetings from Thursday to Sunday. Back then, we couldn't afford to spend much time away from our practices during the week. But when our children were young, we didn't want to spend entire weekends away from home, so we moved away from that schedule.

Now that we have teams in place who can operate our businesses while we are away, we meet during the week. This enables us to spend time with our kids on the weekends.

When you start out, you might be forced to hold meetings on weekends because you don't want to miss a day or two of productive time in the office, when your entire team is there. That was definitely our mind-set early on as well. We were less inclined and less able to miss multiple days in the office back then, before we had "self-managing offices."

We book our meetings several months in advance. We will know the dates of the September meeting before we leave for the March meeting. Otherwise, the meetings will never happen because our schedules fill up quickly. If we don't book it now, it will never happen.

> We book our meetings several months in advance.

Now we are discussing the idea of hosting meetings in

international locations. We've been meeting for twenty years and are just now considering this.

When you first start your study group, it's more important to get to know one another than it is to look for exotic locales in which to hold meetings. We recommend that you spend a couple of years seeing each other's offices, getting to know each other, making sure the chemistry and the culture are compatible, and that you have the right people in place. First, you have to get a good, warm, fuzzy feeling about everybody. Once you have that and are really comfortable that everybody is on the same page, with the same goals and the same dreams, then you can start adding other details. Until you have that, you're spending money or doing something that might be a bit ahead of the curve.

Where to Meet

What has traditionally happened over the years is that one of our meetings each year takes place in the hometown of the person chairing the meeting, and the second meeting of the year takes place at a neutral site. We always try to pick a different neutral site and build activities that tie into that location. We have recently started having meetings at our respective vacation homes.

We typically host one of our meetings in a warm climate. That gives our members from the Midwest a chance to get a break from the cold and snow during the winter.

One of the main reasons for meeting in the chair's hometown is the opportunity to visit that person's office, meet his team, and learn about the processes that go on in his office. A lot of us have redesigned and even built our own offices, so it's helpful to see firsthand how the practices are set up and run. It's critical in the early stages, when you're all just getting to know each other, to visit one another's offices. You learn so much about a person's practice and how he does things by seeing it firsthand and meeting his team.

Setting Rules About Outside Communications and Cell Phones

We don't have any restrictions on the use of technology at our meetings. We try to be respectful of each other and to our speakers by not being on cell phones during presentations, but there are no written, hard-and-fast rules.

We use technology to a great extent, including internet connections, overhead projectors, YouTube videos, and other media that enhance the discussion at hand.

Appointing a Chair

For every meeting we have, we appoint a chair or a czar, and everyone has a turn in that role. We assign an assistant to each meeting, and the chair and assistant put the entire agenda together. They set up the meeting place, organize the outside speaker, and handle all the logistics that are required for a successful meeting. That meeting becomes their own meeting. They might get input from the current members, but they don't necessarily have to. The agenda focuses on topics that are important to all the members. The member who ends up being the chair also calls on his staff members to help put the meeting together.

We have used a couple of different approaches to the organization of meetings. When we were a larger group,

> Each member hosts a meeting every two and a half years.

we had co-chairs. One member handled the logistical planning of the meeting, and another member set the agenda and chose the theme.

As our group became smaller over the years, we have combined those two responsibilities, and one person handles them. With a group of our size, it works out that each member hosts a meeting every two and a half years. We made a conscious decision that the person who is hosting the meeting does everything. If you have a bigger group, you can split up the duties and still not have to do everything for two or three years.

Building the Business Content

We work very hard to make sure the content of our meetings is interesting, helpful, and fun. On Jim Rhome's sports radio show, he has a great expression that we like: "When it's your turn, have a take, but don't suck." We put a lot of time and effort into making sure we are generating great value at every meeting.

Business content can focus on myriad topics. We are constantly learning from each other. For example, we learn which strategies we've put into our respective businesses are the most effective. We will often introduce a topic on an area that we are collectively interested in improving or that's timely.

For example, one big topic on the agenda for a recent meeting concerned a new phenomenon that is being introduced into our industry—robo-advising. With robo-advising, clients would engage with financial advisors through technology, through artificial intelligence. We spent quite a bit of time on this subject, discussing where we think the trend is heading, to what extent it will affect us, what

we think the future will bring, and if we should consider embracing it or at least prepare to address it. And we had a great presentation recently from a high-end professional on learning to become better communicators in our one-on-one relationships with our clients and others. We are always searching for areas in which we can improve.

We have found it to be quite important to have a combination of internal presentations by our group members and by outside professionals. We want to add value by sharing our own ideas, but outside talent is helpful as well.

Bringing in Outside Speakers

We have experienced a gamut of different outside speakers in our group. We normally have multiple outside speakers as a part of each meeting. Some are paid, and sometimes they speak for free. We empower each other to make the decision to hire someone up to a $2,500 maximum for each meeting. If we choose to spend more than that, we bring it to everybody for a quick nod of approval.

> We normally have multiple outside speakers as a part of each meeting.

We have wholesalers come in and speak to our group selectively.

49

We pick those whom we feel can provide some value, who represent a particular product or company. Perhaps it is someone we have worked with in our own region, and we think that person has something that would benefit the group. Speakers are often very eager to come in and present to us to put their companies in a positive light to a highly productive group of producers from around the country. We don't like them to take over our meetings, however, because if the word got out, they would all want to get their time in the spotlight. As a result, we are pretty selective about who we bring in.

A key component to outside speakers is to be sure they do not approach their speaking engagements as opportunities to sell or solicit business. Of course, they need to have some opportunity to connect with us and build rapport, but the focus of their presentations must be informative and educational.

After presentations from outside speakers, we always send them a gift, especially those who gave their time for free. It's very important to thank anybody who spends his or her own time without getting any remuneration. We always send a personalized, significant gift to our speakers to say thanks.

We have visited the offices of speakers who someone in our group knows. For example, we had a winter meeting in Florida, and Ron Greenberg arranged for us to visit with a highly productive organization run by a gentleman named Rick Thomas. He was very gracious and invited us into his office. We saw his operation; we met with his team; and we learned more about his company, his process, and the roles that all his support teammates fill in his organization. It was invaluable to see a team in action on someone's home turf. From an outside-speaker perspective, we don't discriminate. If we think someone can be helpful, we like to invite that person in.

In the early years, a healthy amount of the agenda was filled with our own presentations on concepts and strategies. We were giving more content-oriented feedback to each other in the first five to seven years. Getting feedback on our own individual processes around financial planning, investment management, estate planning, and life insurance was very beneficial.

We spoke about marketing and sales concepts. And we have shared openly how we compensate our teams and structure our bonuses. We spent a fair amount of time, especially in the early days—and on an ongoing basis—on how we pay our staff and on the types of benefits and bonuses we offer.

For example, we would discuss organization charts: "Here's what I'm trying to accomplish. How best do I go about building my team?" We talked about how we compensate dour teams and how we incentivized them with performance-based programs and those types of measuring stakes. We reviewed all the different aspects of how we individually performed the various financial-planning functions, including investment management, estate planning, risk-management planning, and tax analysis.

> It's important to build downtime into your meetings.

The Importance of Including Recreation

In some of our early meetings, we didn't build in much recreation. In hindsight, this was probably a mistake. It's important to build downtime into your meetings so that you don't go, go, go, morning, noon, and night. You must have

some free time to exercise or do a couple of things on your own, whether it's a workout, a walk, or even a nap. During a recent meeting, we went to a baseball game together.

We've found it to be very helpful to have a recreational component to each meeting. It's important to strike a balance between work and recreation. For our group, it has worked well when we've had three-quarters work and one-quarter recreation.

On the recreation side, we always build in enough time to see interesting things in the community we're visiting. Also, we don't skimp on meals. We go to nice restaurants. We treat our teams to experiences that they might not have at home. We build in adequate free time for fitness. We try to make that a priority and live by a whole-person concept. In Minneapolis, we did a fun team-building event called Escape Minnesota, and we went to a Minnesota Twins baseball game on a perfect evening to see a game outside.

We've made it a point to engage in activities we can all do together. For example, we don't all play golf, so we don't play golf during our study-group meetings. If some of us want to do so, we'll come in a day early or stay a day later. John recently took us to the *Maid of the Mist* boat ride under Niagara Falls, a game, and snowmobiling. During other meetings, we attended a wine tasting, heard live music, and took a private bus tour of Nashville.

Follow an Agenda

Following an agenda will keep everyone on track in terms of time spent on various activities. The agenda will be built around the type of meeting: Is it a members-only meeting, a member meeting with associate wealth advisors, a member meeting with an administrative team, or a spousal meeting? The meeting content is directly related to the type of meeting, which we cover in the next chapter. The sample agenda shown here gives you an idea of how we spend our time during a three-day meeting.

Give & Grow Study Group
Lake Geneva, Wisconsin
September 16–18, 2013

Agenda

Monday, September 16th

Arrivals:	Moshides, 7:40 a.m.; Sweet, 8:40 a.m.; Maller and Greenberg to arrive Sunday night; Heckert will pick everyone up at the hotel at 7:10 a.m.
11:30 a.m.	Group lunch
1:00 p.m.	Ron Greenberg presentation; commentary by Peter Maller
3:30 p.m.	Financial planning transitions introduction by Bryan Sweet
4:30 p.m.	Business/personal updates, including:

- Tech ideas – Great iPad apps

- Books – What's the best book you've read this year?
- Social media updates and use
- Google Drive file-sharing website

5:30 p.m.   Relax/exercise
7:00 p.m.   Dinner

Tuesday, September 17th

7:30 a.m.   Breakfast
8:30 a.m.   Session on Vision 2020 – Update on business and personal goals
11:30 a.m. Lunch
1:00 p.m.   Team building: Roundtable discussion on effective business transitions to next generation and how to develop and grow staff
2:30 p.m.   Afternoon of fun: Zipline, boat ride
5:00 p.m.   Relax/exercise, if time permits before dinner
7:00 p.m.   Dinner

Wednesday, September 18th

7:00 a.m.   Breakfast
7:30 a.m.   Presentation: "Bond Alternatives" by James McCuddy with Eaton Vance
9:15 a.m.   Depart for Chicago, Marriott Suites meeting room. Discuss during drive:
- Next meeting: where, when, what, who
- When to include spouses, key employees/partners
- Update from Brian on international speaking opportunities
11:30 a.m. Presentation: "7Twelve Portfolio" by Craig Israelsen, PhD
2:00 p.m.   Working lunch
5:00 p.m.   Departures back to O'Hare

New Feature: A Meeting Archive

Just recently, we decided to add an important new component to our study group. We will hire someone to help our group with logistics. This person will keep track of all our meeting materials on the internet so we can review previous discussions. This person will also help us research meeting locations, book hotels, and handle logistical details so that we don't have to call on our staff members to do all that work. This person will add consistency to each meeting and make sure that any to-do's that come up at a meeting get done and that follow-up calls are scheduled.

> We will hire someone to help our group with logistics.

Depending on how big your group is and how often you meet, chances are that you won't personally have to host meetings that often—maybe once every two years. Put a lot of time, thought, and effort into the meetings you host. Make them memorable and truly useful for your fellow study-group members, and you will all reap the rewards of your well-planned meetings.

CHAPTER 5

Four Types of Meetings

"If you can dream it, you can do it."
—Walt Disney

We discovered early on that we needed to conduct different types of meetings to accomplish different types of tasks. So now, we host four types of meetings.

1. Member Meetings

The first meeting we held, and most of the meetings we still have, are called "member meetings." As the name implies, these meetings are for members only.

These meetings give us an opportunity, because of our close personal relationships, to discuss any topic—any personal issue and anything that could be perceived as confidential as it relates to our personal lives, our business lives, staffing issues, compensation issues, employee incentive programs, etc. These types of issues are on the table for discussion in a members-only meeting.

> We have even shared our personal finances and our personal planning processes.

We have even shared our personal finances and our personal planning processes so we can have the other members critique them. You really know you have the right group when you start to share your most intimate personal information with each other. To do so, you must have a lot of confidence that you have the right people in the group. We evolved to that level of confidence. It wasn't like that in the early years, but that's where we are today.

As mentioned, we often bring in outside speakers to present at our meetings. Some are paid, and some are not. We bring in speakers who specialize in areas we want to focus on or explore. We do our best to stay on the cutting edge of planning concepts and to explore trends in the financial markets. This helps keep us as close to current as we can be so we can provide the best possible advice to our clients.

In these meetings, we also share sales ideas and discuss thoughts for how we want to grow our administrative teams and what their responsibilities are. We discuss issues relating to the industry, cyber-security, quality of life, and work–life balance.

2. Member Meetings with Associate Wealth Advisors

We call the second type of meeting "member meetings with associate wealth advisors." These meetings include the next level of advisors—those who are providing services directly to clients. We initially designed them to develop the knowledge and skills of our advisors and to give them a platform so they could collaborate with each other throughout the year. We discuss, review, or compare their responsibilities.

Some of us have taken in our associate wealth advisors as equity partners and/or have developed a succession plan and put that into place. You can get a sense for how important these meetings have become based on the fact that we have developed this next level of management and have put plans in place for our own successors. We share our individual approaches to common planning concepts. We all tend to use the E-Money Financial Planning System, but each of us presents it in a slightly different way, so we're able to see how everybody uses a similar tool in their practices.

In these meetings, we share portfolio construction ideas, choices of protection products to use, and anything else we think will help us as we give advice to clients throughout the year. Our meetings with associate wealth advisors demonstrate that the Give & Grow Study Group has become bigger than just the five of us. We have a responsibility to our team members and our clients to continue to develop our firms so that we can

> The Give & Grow Study Group has become bigger than just the five of us.

always be on the cutting edge of state-of-the-art financial planning principles that will be shared with our clients.

The well-being of the people in our firms is important to us. When real-life issues arise regarding their responsibilities and challenges, we want to be instrumental in handling them in the best way possible. The study group is a great forum in which to discuss these situations.

3. Administrative Meetings

The third type of study group meeting we call "administrative meetings." They include our top administrative folks, who are responsible for running the operations of our offices. The focus of these meetings is on a whole different end of running a financial services practice. We discuss ways to improve the processing of paperwork, technology, and personnel management. Administrative meetings focus on people, paper flow, cyber-security issues, and personnel situations.

Administrative meetings focus on people, paper flow, cyber-security issues, and personnel situations.

60

We regularly have outsiders come in to facilitate these meetings. These are usually professionals who have personal experience with the challenges of running the administrative side of a busy financial services firm. They know what services the offices are providing, but they're also educated on compliance and other issues that are becoming more significant. This helps us learn how to implement whatever controls are necessary.

A primary benefit to bringing our staff to the meetings is that doing so results in faster and greater buy-in from our teams, which allows us to become successful faster. The team is the big engine that keeps everything running. We are the visionaries, so our team members have to understand why we're doing everything we're doing. By coming to these meetings, our teams grasp the vision much faster and understand it better. And they become our partners in executing that vision.

Including our staff in the study group meetings has been hugely effective on many levels:

- Staff members have observed firsthand the camaraderie and impact we have derived from the meetings.
- They feel special and valued because we are making an investment in them and their futures.
- It demonstrates that we believe they are a vital part of our futures.
- Staff members learn, give, and grow as a result of the interactions they have with us and with each other.

Normally, each study-group member brings one to two people to these meetings. They all have different titles: office manager, chief

Normally, each study-group member brings one to two people to these meetings.

operating officer, support administrator, and the like. We all make the individual decision of who we think would benefit most from being at our administrative meetings.

4. Spousal Meetings

The fourth meeting is the "spousal meeting." At first, we weren't sure if bringing our spouses to the meetings was a good idea because there was a little bit of risk associated with bringing our spouses together. However, we thought it would be an opportunity to continue to have a business meeting and to see if we could develop some camaraderie among our wives.

We have now held spousal meetings multiple times, and it has been amazing to observe the close, personal relationships that are developing as our wives become more comfortable with each other and get to know each other's personalities, likes, and dislikes.

Our spousal meetings incorporate business discussions, similar to our members-only meetings, with fun spousal activities. We've been to Broadway shows in New York City. We've gone up in a hot-air balloon in California. We've been to Florida, and we've been to Canyon Ranch, which is a unique physical-fitness experience. We always include nice dinners during these meetings.

Not only have our spouses gotten close as a result of our including them, but we know more about each other's families. It has brought us even closer at a whole new level.

Communicating Between Meetings

> "One thing we will not be around this office is lazy."
> —John C. Moshides

We make it a point to stay in touch between meetings with thoughts, ideas, questions, and comments. We do this via email, conference calls, and WebEx software.

Between meetings, we share ideas for meeting locations, speakers, agendas, food, and fun. We like to think big and outside the box when planning the meetings.

We—not just us, but our team members and spouses as well—maintain common values and live by them. We act as each other's board of directors, not just during our meetings but between meetings as well.

You can see how well an effective study group can develop and the impact it can have on so many different people and levels within your firm and your family.

CHAPTER 6

Managing Expenses

> "You cannot have million-dollar dreams with penny thoughts."
> —Brian Heckert

We run our study group like a business. With any business, it's important to have ground rules for certain expenses so there are no misunderstandings. At the end of this chapter, we've included a sample spreadsheet we use to help keep track of expenses and calculations. We have customized an Excel spreadsheet that makes the calculations very easy, even if we have accumulated a lot of receipts over several days. It keeps the bookkeeping hassle to a minimum.

When we first started the group, we decided to share the travel expenses equally. If one group member has a short trip with a short, inexpensive flight, he will share the financial burden of another group member who has to take a very expensive flight to get to the same meeting. Our philosophy is that the common expenses of putting

> **The common expenses should be shared equally.**

on the meeting and getting to the meeting, as well as housing and meals, should be shared equally, no matter where you are in the country. We share expenses related to airfare, hotel rooms, and common meals.

If we bring guests to the meeting, whether they are staff members or spouses, we split off individual expenses by office.

If one advisor wants to bring three members of his firm to the meeting, and another member wants to bring only one, we use a multiplier to break up the costs per attendee, and then each office pays its fair share, depending on how many people attended.

Sharing expenses has allowed us to plan where we want our meetings to be held unselfishly. This enables us to derive the maximum impact from a meeting without worrying whether somebody is always getting a deal or a discount on the travel.

One of the choices you will want to consider is how your group wants to handle situations like the consumption of liquor during recreational activities. It's important to set ground rules early on. Those can be either shared or individual expenses. There is no right or wrong answer here, as long as everybody knows the expectations beforehand.

There will be recreational expenses to consider as well. If you have physical limitations in a group, where part of the party is going off to do some kind of physical exercise that others are incapable of doing, ground rules at the beginning will help determine how those expenses should be handled. Does someone share in the expense of an activity if he can't participate? Each study group has to come up with its own answers because each group will have different priorities and concerns.

We recommend that you have a written policy in the form of a handbook or reference guide, especially in a new study group. Make sure everyone understands the rules for spending and for dividing expenses.

Sample Expense Spreadsheet

Expense	Amount
Mileage @ $0.55	
Airfare	
Car rental/gas	
Lodging rooms	
Misc.	
Meeting rooms	$2,400
Speaker fee	2,500
Gift card for speaker	100
Hilton – drinks	
Dinners	2,350
Ball game	950
Escape MSP	550
Train fare	40
Total	**$8,890**

The bottom line is, establish ground rules when you first establish your group. Make sure everyone agrees on them, and make sure you communicate them effectively in writing and that all group members follow them consistently. Ensuring that expenses are handled equitably will go a long way toward building trust among study-group members.

CHAPTER 7

Where We Go from Here

> "True humility is not thinking less of yourself;
> it is thinking of yourself less."
> —C. S. Lewis

Now that we have two decades of giving, growth, and success behind us, where do we go from here? The truth is, from the very beginning, our study group has been a constant evolution. We hope the group continues to push us forward and that we keep challenging each other to grow, to be on the cutting edge, and to break out of our comfort zones.

We each work hard to maintain a high level of courage. Courage leads to growth because you learn new strategies and concepts when you are always turning over another rock or taking another step into turbulent water. We give each other the confidence to do that, and, as a result, we continue to develop new capabilities within our firms.

Into uncharted waters is where we are going to go from

here. We continue as a group to be excited, both about our group and about the quality of services we provide to our clients in this ever-changing world. We are better leaders as a result of spending the time and effort to be together, twice a year, and all the support we give each other in between. Striving to improve constantly is not about *perfection*; it's about *progress*. For us, the study group means continuing to progress and improve.

We now have mature practices, and we realize that we have worked hard to develop the roles and identities of others within our practices. The less important we, as principals, become to the success of our firms, the better off the firms will be, the better off our clients will be, and probably the better the value of our practices will be. This means that the group has caused us to develop great depth and great quality of talent beneath us.

> The group has caused us to develop great depth and great quality of talent beneath us.

We live by the basic principle that we will always have a bigger future if we pay attention and have positive attitudes. We are all committed to our clients, the companies we represent, and our employees. We are always filled with ideas that excite us, and we're starting to branch into new areas, like writing this book. That's a bold move for us. Not only are we writing this book collectively, but we're all branching off and writing individual books as well. Some of us have visions of developing companies or services that can be provided to other financial services organizations because of what we've learned and what we've built.

You can see how our Give & Grow Study Group has evolved from a bunch of guys getting together to improve as professionals to a group of experienced practice owners with mature businesses. It is important for all of us that we impact

BENCHMARK

our communities in significant ways, through charitable giving and other exciting endeavors. We see a very big and bright future, but a changing future, for all of us, based on a lot of personal factors that are starting to show up.

If you are thinking about starting a brand-new study group, we highly encourage you to put in place a mechanism to benchmark your results every third or fifth year. That way, you can watch, monitor, and evaluate the progress of the group and chronicle the "A-ha!" moments you experience together.

It has been an enlightening exercise to benchmark our production and incomes and to document the ideas that came from the study group that created turning points at which our practices took completely unexpected turns.

The best practices we have shared in this book have kept our group going for two decades and growing to the point that we can't imagine running our firms without it. Our greatest wish for you is that participation in your study group gives you as much meaning and joy as we have received from being members of ours. Here's to your success!

About the Authors

Ronald J. Greenberg, CLU®, AEP®

Founding Partner
Greenberg & Rapp Financial Group, Inc.
M Holdings Securities, Inc.
East Hanover, New Jersey
rgreenberg@greenbergandrapp.com
www.greenbergandrapp.com

Founding Partner Ronald Greenberg has devoted his practice to working with closely held business owners and affluent individuals. He has developed one of the leading national firms dedicated to helping clients grow, manage, and protect their wealth.

Ron began his financial services career in 1988. He first qualified for the prestigious Million Dollar Round Table in 1991 and has been a Top of the Table-level advisor for the past fifteen years. He holds the Chartered Life Underwriter (CLU®) and Accredited Estate Planners (AEP®) designations and is a past president of the North Jersey Chapter of the Society of Financial Service Professionals. He is also a member of the Tri-County and Northern New Jersey Estate Planning Councils. He speaks extensively on the topics of preserving family wealth and exit-planning strategies for business owners.

In his community, Ron is a founding board member of Liam's Room, whose mission is to create home-like hospital rooms for children with life-threatening illnesses. He is a board member for Cerebral Palsy of North Jersey.

Ron is an avid golfer and lives in Westfield, New Jersey, with his wife, Debbie, and their two children.

Brian D. Heckert, CLU®, ChFC®, QPFC, AIF®

CEO and Founder
Financial Solutions Midwest, LLC
Kestra Investment Services, LLC
Nashville, Illinois
bheckert@401knowhow.com
www.financialsolutionsmidwest.com

Financial Solutions Midwest, LLC
Financial Solutions From Trusted Advisors

Brian entered a career in finance in 1985 and is a successful business leader in southwestern Illinois. He focuses his practice on retirement plan administration and business planning.

As a Managing Member of Financial Solutions Midwest, LLC, Brian dedicates his professional life to providing strategic advice and services for individuals and businesses. His firm focuses on qualified plans, business planning, and asset management. His clients are business owners with first-generation wealth located throughout the Midwest.

In 2016, Brian served as 90th president of the Million Dollar Round Table (MDRT), the premier association of financial professionals worldwide.

His MDRT volunteerism has included speaking at the MDRT Annual Meeting and MDRT Experience Meeting and serving on multiple MDRT committees and task forces over the past twenty-five years. He served on the

MDRT Foundation Board of Trustees and the 2010 Annual Meeting and Membership Division in 2012. He was also the Divisional Vice President and Divisional Vice President of Program General Arrangements. He is a twenty-seven-year MDRT member and holds several professional merits, including seven Court of the Table and eight Top of the Table qualifications. Also, he has been involved in the creation of the Annual Meeting Connexion Zone and Resource Zone.

In addition, Brian is a Legion of Honor Excalibur Knight-level donor of the MDRT Foundation, the philanthropic arm of MDRT. He is also a member of the organization's Inner Circle Society, a distinguished group of donors who have supported the MDRT Foundation.

Brian is a local member of the Nashville Lions, the Chamber of Commerce, and St. Ann's Catholic Church.

Peter D. Maller,
MBA, CFP®, AEP®

Founder and President
Maller Wealth Advisors, Inc.
Lincoln Financial Advisors
Hunt Valley, Maryland
Peter.Maller@LFG.com
mallerwealthadvisors.com

Peter has more than twenty-five years of experience in the financial planning industry and specializes in working with successful business owners, professionals, and high-net-worth individuals throughout the United States.

He was named the Lincoln Financial Network (LFN) Planner of the Year in 2007, every year from 2009 to 2014, 2016, and 2017. He was recognized in the August 2011 issue of *Registered Rep* magazine as one of America's Top 100 Independent B/D Advisors (#18). He was named among *Barron's* Top 1200 Advisors and *The Daily Record's* 2016 and 2017 "Most Admired CEOs."

His firm, Maller Wealth Advisors, was named as a 2015 and 2016 winner of *Inc. Magazine's* Top 5000 list of Fastest-Growing Private Companies in America. Peter is also a qualified member of the prestigious Million Dollar Round Table and has achieved Top of the Table status, ranking him in the top half of the top 1 percent of advisors in the industry. For more information regarding these awards, go to http://mallerwealthadvisors.com/2017/08/08/awards-recognitions-2.

He completed his undergraduate degree at Washington College, graduating magna cum laude, and earned his Master of Business Administration degree from Florida State University. A two-time collegiate tennis All-American, Peter continues to be an active member in the Maryland athletic community.

He is a **CERTIFIED FINANCIAL PLANNER™ Professional**, having earned his designation through the College for Financial Planning, and is certified as an **ACCREDITED ESTATE PLANNER** Designee by the National Association of Estate Planners & Councils. He is FINRA Series 6, 7, 63, and 65 registered and Life, Accident and Health insurance licensed.

Peter is a true leader in giving back and supports more than twenty different charities and not-for-profit organizations, both nationally and internationally. His community involvement includes serving on the Board of Trustees at The Baltimore Estate Planning Council, the Board of Trustees at Garrison Forest School, the Washington College President's Leadership Council, and the Parents' Council at Miami University of Ohio.

In 2016 and 2017, Peter was the presenting sponsor for the Stroup Kids for Kids Epilepsy cause. He also gives his time to his alma maters. At Washington College, he has served on many different committees and received the distinguished Alumni Service Award in recognition of his involvement and support. He has served on the MBA Advisory Board for Florida State University.

John C. Moshides, CLU®, ChFC®, AEP®, CLTC®

Financial Services Executive
President, Moshides Financial Group
Creator of The Wealth Management
    Process™ and The Business of Wealth
MML Investors Services, LLC
Amherst, New York
john@moshidesfinancial.com
www.moshidesfinancial.com

Moshides Financial Group
Your Guide to Financial Security

John Moshides focuses on helping successful people with the accumulation, management, and preservation of their wealth.

A native of Niagara Falls, New York, John earned a bachelor's degree in management from The State University of New York at Buffalo in 1980. He started his financial services career in 1981. In 1987, he founded Moshides Financial Group, Inc., offering a full spectrum of financial planning services. He earned his Chartered Life Underwriter designation in 1991 and became certified in Long Term Care planning in 2005. John earned his Chartered Financial Consultant designation in 2010 and also was certified as an Accredited Estate Planner.

John is a past president of the Buffalo Chapter of the Society of Financial Service Professionals and is one of only a few recipients of the Distinguished Service Award from the Society. He is a Qualifying and Life Member of the Million Dollar Round Table, with many Top of the Table and Court of the Table qualifications.

He is a past president of the National Association of Insurance and Financial Advisors – Buffalo Chapter. He is currently a Board Member of Estate Analysts of Western New York. He is an involved member of his community and an active member of St. George Eastern Orthodox Church.

John resides in Clarence, New York, with his wife, Suzanne, and their daughters, Dana and Lindsay.

Bryan J. Sweet,
CLU®, ChFC®, MSFS, CFS®

Founder and CEO, Sweet Financial
   Services
Wealth Advisor, Raymond James
   Financial Services
Raymond James Financial Services, Inc.
Creator of The Dream Architect™
Cofounder of Dare to Dream
   Enterprises
Creator of Elite Wealth Advisor
   Symposium
Fairmont, Minnesota
Bryan@sweetfinancial.com
www.sweetfinancial.com

Sweet Financial
services

Since the start of his financial services career in 1979, Bryan Sweet has specialized in helping individuals accumulate and preserve wealth for retirement and beyond. A native of Fairmont, Minnesota, he earned his master's degree in financial services from The American College in Bryn Mawr, Pennsylvania, before embarking on what would become a lifelong career as a wealth management consultant.

In 1987, Bryan established Sweet Financial Services and developed an alliance with Raymond James Financial Services in 1989. Bryan has been a member of the Raymond James Chairman's Council since 2004.*

Bryan's drive and relentless pursuit to simplify, inspire, and improve the future of his practice's clients has given him and his team the opportunity to be recognized in industry publications, such as being named to the *Inc.* Magazine Top 5000 list for fastest-growing private companies since 2014.** To continue to provide the best client experience possible, Bryan has made the commitment to participate in the Ed Slott Top Advisor Group, Peak Advisor Alliance, The Genius Network, and the Strategic Coach Program.

It is because of Bryan's passion in working with his best clients—high-net-worth business owners with complex financial needs—that he decided to develop Dare to Dream Enterprises. The organization helps provide clarity in a world of chaos so that people can dream bigger dreams and focus on the things in life that matter most to them. Dare to Dream supports business owners, women in transition, and others who are looking to build a bigger future and take control of their lives.

Locally, Bryan's passion for creating a greater community shines through as being part of the Fairmont Opera House Endowment Committee and the Martin County Area Foundation. He is a past chairman of the board of the Fairmont Area Chamber of Commerce.

Bryan and his wife, Mary Beth, live in Fairmont. Bryan recently established the *Marilyn Sweet-Borchardt Education Foundation* in honor of his mother to help single women who have children going to college. Currently, the foundation is helping support two young people each year, and as the fund grows, more grants will be provided.

*Membership is based on prior fiscal year production. Requalification is required annually.

**The ranking of *Inc.* Magazine's Inc. 5000 list is based on the percentage of revenue growth over a three-year period. To qualify, companies must have been founded and generating revenue by March 31, 2013. They had to be US-based, privately held, for profit, and independent—not subsidiaries or divisions of other companies. The minimum revenue required for 2013 was $100,000; the minimum revenue requirement since inception of this recognition has been increased each year. *Inc.* Magazine reserves the right to decline applicants for subjective reasons. This award

Contact Us

Please visit www.giveandgrowstudygroup.com to do the following:

- Book the Give & Grow Study Group members as speakers at your next meeting. We can do presentations and host workshops to help you launch your own study group or refine an existing group.

- Obtain resources to help you establish a study group.

- Request more in-depth guidance on specific aspects of starting and maintaining a study group.

- Suggest additional topics we can include in future updates of this book that you would find helpful. We welcome and value your input!

Broker Dealer Affiliations and Disclosure

Ron Greenberg: M Holdings Securities, Inc.

Brian Heckert: Kestra Investment Services, LLC, is not affiliated with any other entity listed. This book is for information purposes. It is not intended for financial or investment advice and is not a solicitation to offer or sell securities. Kestra Investment Services, LLC, is not responsible for the content of any website or the collection or use of information regarding any website's users and/or members.

Peter Maller: Lincoln Financial Advisors (Lincoln Financial Advisors and Peter are not affiliated with any of the other broker dealers listed in this book.)

John Moshides: MML Investors Services, LLC

Bryan Sweet: Raymond James Financial Services, Inc.

Any opinions are those of Bryan Sweet and not necessarily those of Raymond James.

Sweet Financial Services is not a registered broker/dealer and is independent of Raymond James Financial Services. Investment advisory services offered through Raymond James Financial Services Advisors, Inc. Securities offered through Raymond James Financial Services, Inc. Member FINRA/SIPC. Raymond James is not affiliated with any of the individuals and/or their organizations named herein this book.

Made in the USA
Columbia, SC
31 May 2019